The Campus History Series

UNIVERSITY OF DENVER

On the Front Cover: Square dancing with a Western flair was popular at the University of Denver in the 1940s and 1950s. The Square-Dancing Club began in 1938. From 1941 to 1947, the group was known as the Pioneer Promenaders; in 1948, the name was changed to the Dudes and Dames. Shown here are six students from the Dudes and Dames dancing outside on the Mary Reed Library balcony with a view of the mountains in the background. The women are wearing long dresses, while the men are wearing cowboy boots. (University of Denver Archives.)

Cover Background: Four students of the University of Denver are looking out over the mountain range from a Denver mountain parks road around 1920. (University of Denver Archives.)

The Campus History Series

UNIVERSITY OF DENVER

STEVE FISHER AND THYRIA K. WILSON

ARCADIA PUBLISHING

ISBN 978-1-4671-2853-7

Published by Arcadia Publishing
Charleston, South Carolina

Printed in the United States of America

Library of Congress Control Number: 2017955312

For all general information, please contact Arcadia Publishing:
Telephone 843-853-2070
Fax 843-853-0044
E-mail sales@arcadiapublishing.com
For customer service and orders:
Toll-Free 1-888-313-2665

Visit us on the Internet at www.arcadiapublishing.com

To Katie.

—Steve Fisher

In memory of my mother, Lois R. Wescott, who was a geology graduate student at DU.

—Thyria Kathleen Wilson

CONTENTS

ACKNOWLEDGMENTS

We wish to thank Dean Michael Levine-Clark and Jack Maness at the University Libraries, University of Denver, and Dr. Jeanne Abrams, director of the Rocky Mountain Jewish Historical Society and Beck Archives, Special Collections, Center for Judaic Studies and University Libraries, for their assistance and the use of images from the special collections and archives. Thanks also to Jim Kroll and Coi Drummond-Gehrig of the Western History Department of the Denver Public Library for locating and for granting use of hard-to-find images. Special thanks to Sara Schaller for her assistance in all aspects of this book. Thanks to Emily Kintigh for finding some wonderful images, to Doug Rippey for his invaluable research abilities, to Carolyn Cavicchio for her assistance on editing and locating photographs of the Colorado Woman's College (CWC), and to the university photographer, Wayne Armstrong, for taking some beautiful photographs. We also wish to thank our editor at Arcadia Publishing, Liz Gurley, for all her expert guidance and assistance. Unless otherwise noted, all photographs are courtesy of Special Collections, University Libraries, University of Denver.

INTRODUCTION

Gold was discovered in Colorado in 1858, and the "Pikes Peak or Bust!" gold rush was in full force by the next year. When John Evans arrived in Denver to become the territorial governor in 1862, there were still many shacks, log cabins, saloons, and teepees at the confluence of Cherry Creek and the South Platte River in the town of 3,000 citizens. A fire burned much of the business district in 1863, and the next year, a flash flood swept down Cherry Creek, again destroying much of the downtown area.

So that students would not need to "make a pilgrimage to the States" back east, Gov. John Evans developed a plan to bring higher education to people in the Rocky Mountains region. On March 5, 1864, Governor Evans signed the charter for the Colorado Seminary, a coeducational institution of higher learning that required no religious test, although the seminary began as a Methodist school. The first building was erected that same year at Fourteenth and Arapahoe Streets, next to the Evans home. A fire in 1866 in the seminary building belfry caused a substantial amount of damage, much of it done by members of the volunteer fire department, who enthusiastically threw books and furniture out the windows. This was the impetus for Denver quickly founding a professional fire department.

The Sand Creek Massacre took place on November 29, 1864. Governor Evans had established an Indian-fighting regiment under Col. John Chivington. Colonel Chivington attacked peaceful Southern Cheyenne and Arapaho villages, killing over 160 women, children, and the elderly. Public outcry led Pres. Andrew Johnson to ask Governor Evans to resign. Evans would still chair the seminary board until his death in 1897.

The Colorado Seminary closed in late 1867, and John Evans purchased the original building to save it from foreclosure. In 1880, the seminary opened again as the University of Denver, with stronger ties to Denver and weaker ones with the Methodist Church. John Evans donated 10 lots at Fourteenth and Arapahoe Streets. The University of Denver (DU) opened with 30 students from primary grades to college level. It started with the College of Liberal Arts, the College of Music, the College of Fine Arts, and the Colorado Seminary. The frontier needed doctors, and the Medical Department was instituted in 1881. After a two-year course for a doctor of medicine degree, five students received their credentials in 1883. Degrees in music and art were awarded after four years of study. The first year ended with a total enrollment of 150 students, most in preparatory programs.

The College of Law opened in 1892, and the charter included the directive that women were to be "entitled to all privileges." The first woman law graduate was Ann Hunt in 1894. Mary Florence Lathrop graduated in 1896 and was the first woman to argue before the

Colorado Supreme Court. In 1904, the College of Law began the Legal Aid Dispensary, pairing law students with clients who could not afford an attorney. The legislature had enacted a student practice law that allowed law students to practice in state courts. The College of Law merged with the Westminster College of Law in 1957 and continued that school's night program. The night program had begun in 1912 and was the only night program west of the Mississippi until 1920.

The university was successful in downtown Denver, but Denver's population grew to 40,000, and the downtown area was filled with pollution, noise, and many saloons and brothels. The leaders of the College of Liberal Arts decided to move their school to a pastoral setting that was more conducive to academic study. The doctors, dentists, lawyers, artists, musicians, businessmen, and librarians remained downtown. In 1940, the university moved the law school to the University Park campus. It was a disaster, as enrollment plunged to only eight students, and in 1945, the law school was again located downtown. When expansion was needed for the downtown campus, additional buildings were constructed using the proceeds of the sale of the Haish building.

Rufus "Potato" Clark and a group of farmers offered to gift 150 acres for a new campus about five miles southeast of downtown Denver. Clark, a reformed alcoholic who was saved at a revival meeting, made the offer conditional on the school planting trees and instituting an alcohol ban. Within a short time, the new campus grew to nearly 500 acres that featured more jackrabbits and coyotes than people. In 1890, University Hall was built, and in 1892, the College of Liberal Arts was officially relocated to the new University Park campus. It would be 10 years before electricity was installed in the area.

The silver panic of 1893 brought new financial problems to the university. University Hall was in danger of being sold to house a glue factory. Faculty were often paid in livestock or land. Henry Augustus Buchtel, a Methodist minister, became chancellor in 1900. He was known for his fundraising abilities, although he preferred teaching. Once, when a young boy swallowed a quarter, someone shouted "Go get Chancellor Buchtel! If he can't get the quarter out of him, nobody can!" Buchtel was able to pay off all debts by 1906, and several new buildings were added while he was chancellor. He also began a Saturday College for teachers and "workingman's lectures." In 1919, the Denver Presbytery labeled DU and Iliff School of Theology as "hotbeds of infidelity" because some faculty were teaching Darwinism. Buchtel retorted that his faculty and students had complete religious freedom and declared that the university was nonsectarian.

Colorado Woman's College (CWC) was conceived as a "Vassar of the West" by its founder, the Rev. Robert Cameron, pastor of the First Baptist Church of Denver, who wanted to establish a women's college in the western United States that would offer high-level academic courses to women. The college was incorporated in 1888, though CWC did not open until 1909. Treat Hall was the first building on the campus, which was four miles east of Denver on an open prairie in what became the city's Park Hill neighborhood. In 1982, faced with declining enrollment, increasing debt, and an aging physical plant, CWC was acquired by DU, which kept the CWC Weekend College. The Lowell Thomas Law Building was built on the Park Hill (CWC) campus in 1983 to house DU's College of Law, and the DU Lamont School of Music moved to the campus in 1985. The Weekend College was renamed The Women's College in 1993 and continued to operate on the Park Hill campus until 2001, when it moved to the University Park campus. After the Park Hill campus was fully acquired by Johnson & Wales University in 2004, Lamont School of Music and the College of Law moved to new buildings at the University Park campus. The acquisition of CWC almost bankrupted DU again, and faculty and staff were cut, but the university managed to bounce back once again and expand.

One

Downtown Denver and Civic Center Campus

When territorial governor John Evans proposed the idea of creating an institution of higher learning for the Rocky Mountain region, Denver was a frontier town of 3,000 people, mostly men. It seemed an impossible goal, but the Methodists decided that it could be done. The Colorado Seminary began life in a brick building next to the Evans home at Fourteenth and Arapahoe Streets. The college opened for classes in 1864 with three departments: primary, preparatory, and academic. Within a few years, John Evans had to rescue the building from foreclosure. The seminary reopened as the University of Denver in 1880 with the assistance of people in Denver. John Hipp, the first liberal arts student, received a degree in 1884. The Haish Manual Training Building and the Denver Conservatory of Music were also established at Fourteenth and Arapahoe Streets. The university included the College of Liberal Arts, College of Fine Arts, College of Law, preparatory departments, and the Medical Department.

When the wildness of frontier Denver began encroaching on the small university, the leaders decided to move the College of Liberal Arts three miles southeast of Denver. When the Haish building was sold, the Civic Center campus was created, and new buildings were opened closer to the Colorado Capitol and the Denver City and County Building. The College of Law and Lamont School of Music moved to the former Colorado Woman's College campus in 1983 before moving to the University Park campus by 2004.

The home of Gov. John Evans was located at Fourteenth and Arapahoe Streets, and the Colorado Seminary started on the same block. The Denver Center for the Performing Arts is now at this location. This view shows a rough dirt street, buildings, and trees, with a horse and buggy on the left side of the street and four wagons on the right side, including a buckboard and delivery wagon.

In 1864, the simple Colorado Seminary brick building was completed next to the Evans home on Fourteenth Street. Sometimes classrooms were used to teach four classes or grades simultaneously. There are women and children and a few men standing in front of the building, and a man and five women stand on a balcony. (Courtesy of the Denver Public Library, Western History Collection, WH2129.)

John Hipp left the hard labor of his family farm and went to Denver. He asked Chancellor David Hastings Moore for help to enter college. Moore hired Hipp as a janitor and steward in the boarding department. Hipp, a Catholic, was the first and only liberal arts graduate in 1884. He graduated from the DU College of Law in 1894 and was a successful attorney until his death in 1928.

In April 1909, Prof. Herbert A. Howe (with beard at center) and his engineering students set the mile-high bronze benchmark on the steps of the state capitol building. Surveying equipment shown includes transits, stadia rods, measuring tapes, and boxes for the instruments. Professor Howe filled many roles at DU, including astronomer at the Chamberlin Observatory. (Courtesy of the Denver Public Library, Western History Collection, WH2129.)

This view is looking down Fourteenth Street toward Arapahoe Street. The Haish building is on the left, and the Denver Conservatory of Music is on the right. The Denver Conservatory of Music became the DU School of Music in 1898, which was discontinued in 1911, although some music classes continued. The Department of Music was established in 1935 and merged into the Lamont School of Music in 1942.

Barbed-wire magnate Jacob Haish wanted to ensure that young people had a place to further their knowledge of the manual arts, and financed a program and building from half of his barbed-wire sales in Colorado, Wyoming, Utah, and New Mexico. The Haish building later housed the law school, dental, pharmacy, and medical colleges, and the School of Commerce.

The Haish School of Manual Training opened in 1887 as a high school with 11 students, designed to train boys in a skilled trade and teach them the dignity of manual labor. The manual training high school was discontinued in 1892, when East High began a similar training program. The three students standing in the machine shop are 1890 graduates of DU.

Women and a few men are pictured working at stations in the carpentry shop in the Haish building. Some of the women students are being taught how to complete various woodworking projects. The women toward the front of the room are wearing aprons and working on woodcarving, and tools are hanging from pegboards in the room. Both women and men needed carpentry skills.

Blacksmiths were valued on the frontier to fix buggies, wagons, farm and ranch equipment, and even horseshoes. The Haish School of Manual Training included facilities to teach this craft. Forge stations are set up in the interior of this windowless wood structure, and anvils, places for coal fires, iron tools, and large hoods are at each station.

When the university was reorganized in 1880, the decision was made to remain in the same location at Fourteenth and Arapahoe Streets and just add to the old building. The new building included a new story added onto the original seminary building and the additions of the Boys' Hall of four stories along Arapahoe Street and the Girls' Department of four stories along Fourteenth Street.

The Denver Conservatory of Music was established in 1887 and became the DU School of Music in 1898, although music classes were given intermittently in the 1910s. A music degree required four years of study, and the conservatory was located in the "new" building. The Lamont School of Music, located near downtown at 909 Grant Avenue, was purchased by DU in 1932. In 1941, the University of Denver School of Music and the Lamont School of Music merged.

The first chancellor and first faculty of the University of Denver in 1880 are shown here. From left to right are Sidney H. Short, Herbert A. Howe, Chancellor David Hastings Moore, O.B. Super, and Frances Fish. Dr. Howe taught mathematics and astronomy and was later concurrently director of the Chamberlain Observatory, dean of the College of Liberal Arts, and dean of the Graduate College throughout most of the 1890s.

A man sits in the instrumental room of the Denver Conservatory of Music. A piano and an organ are shown, but other instruments that were portable would also be played in this room. The instrumental room was used for studying and practicing on various instruments. There was a separate room for vocal lessons and practice.

Nine women are sitting or standing around a piano in the vocal department of the Denver Conservatory of Music. Singing was taught in the vocal department, and small concerts were also held in this room. The Denver Conservatory of Music was changed to the DU School of Music in 1898. Emma Azalia Hackley, who earned a music degree in 1900, was the first African American to graduate from DU.

Eight women are sitting and one woman is standing in the vocal room of the Denver Conservatory of Music. The piano would be used to set the melody and to accompany singers. Music and art were popular classes for refined young women. This photograph would have been taken before 1898, when the DU School of Music was created.

The University of Denver Women's Glee Club members are pictured in matching blouses and skirts. One woman is holding a guitar, one holds a violin, and four hold mandolins. The image dates from the early 1900s. The first college glee clubs began in England in 1787, the word "glee" referring to short English part songs. Glee clubs became very popular in American high schools.

The Lamont School of Music, located at 909 Grant Street, is shown after it was purchased by DU in 1941. The school was founded in 1924 by Florence Lamont Hinman as a private proprietary school and flourished during the 1920s and 1930s. After the merger, the combined schools remained under the direction of Florence Hinman until she retired in 1952.

The original downtown campus at Fourteenth and Arapahoe Streets became overcrowded, even with the transfer of liberal arts courses to University Park in 1890. The professional schools prospered in the bustling central business district. The School of Commerce, Accounts, and Finance began in the Haish building in 1908. At first, students attended classes three nights a week. In 1922, the School of Commerce moved to Twentieth Street and Glenarm Place.

Mary Florence Lathrop, shown in 1900, graduated first in her class in 1896 from the College of Law. She was the first woman admitted to the US District Court and to argue before the Colorado Supreme Court. She was known as "that damn woman" by some opposing lawyers. One of the cases she won established the law of charitable bequests. (Courtesy of the Denver Public Library, Western History Collection, WH2129.)

A coeducational class in the University Shorthand School at the downtown campus is shown holding pads of paper and pencils for practicing shorthand in 1891. This was a skill useful in many types of work. Court stenographers, secretaries, and most office clerks were required to known shorthand. Secretarial and clerical positions were considered suitable for single women.

This Arapahoe Street view includes the Denver and Gross College of Medicine (the DU medical school) the laboratory building, the dispensary, the first university building, and the Haish building. Neither the University of Denver medical school nor the University of Colorado (CU) Medical School could pass the standards of the American Medical Association independently. The two schools merged in 1912 to become the CU Medical School in Denver.

The dispensary and laboratory buildings of the Denver and Gross College of Medicine were on Arapahoe Street. The Medical Department of the University of Denver, established in 1881, merged with its competitor, Gross Medical College, to form the Denver and Gross College of Medicine in 1903. By 1889, the DU Medical Department had graduated 42 physicians.

Dr. Charles Spivak served as an associate professor in the Medical Department at the University of Denver from 1896 to 1901, as a professor of anatomy in 1897–1898, and as the chair of gastroenterology at the Medical Department. Dr. Spivak (second from rear, seated at desk) is pictured in the office of the Jewish Consumptives' Relief Society, formed in 1905 to treat tuberculosis victims. (Courtesy of Beck Archives, Special Collections, University of Denver.)

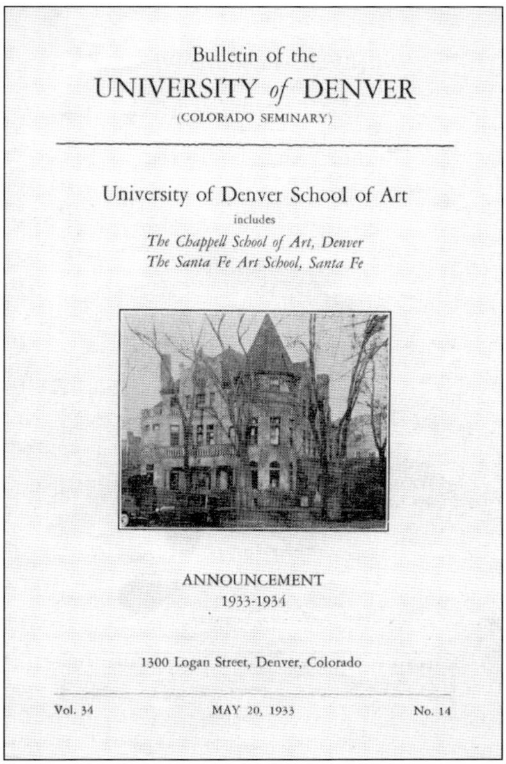

Bulletin of the

UNIVERSITY *of* DENVER

(COLORADO SEMINARY)

University of Denver School of Art

includes

The Chappell School of Art, Denver

The Santa Fe Art School, Santa Fe

ANNOUNCEMENT

1933-1934

1300 Logan Street, Denver, Colorado

Vol. 34 MAY 20, 1933 No. 14

The 1933–1934 bulletin of the University of Denver School of Art announced that the School of Art included the Chappell School of Art in Denver and the Santa Fe Art School in New Mexico. The first two floors of the Chappell mansion at 1300 Logan Street in downtown Denver were used by the Denver Art Museum, and the top floor was used as art studios by DU.

Drawing and painting classes were available at extra cost at the DU School of Art and were considered a proper exercise for the leisure time of young ladies. Anne Evans, daughter of John Evans, was an early member of the Denver Artists' Club, which later became the Denver Art Museum. She was a major collector of Pueblo art, which she donated to the museum.

In 1929, artist Vance Kirkland (not pictured), famous for his avant-garde style, became the founding director of the art department. He left DU in 1932 over a salary dispute and began his own very successful art school. Kirkland returned to DU as director in 1946 at a salary equal to the chancellor and brought 200 students from his school with him. When he retired in 1969, there were 400 art majors.

In the 1950s, DU art students are drawing a triangular-shaped draped object in front of a backdrop. Under the direction of Vance Kirkland (upper right), still art moved from traditional still life objects to more abstract objects. The Kirkland Museum of Fine and Decorative Arts in Denver contains many Kirkland paintings as one of its three collecting areas.

Art students watch an art professor draw a portrait of a student. Another student appears to be looking at something else. Inattentive students would not have pleased Vance Kirkland. He had no patience for mediocrity or for students who would not work. He once sent a student in search of "vanishing points" so the student could erase mistakes. Nevertheless, his classes were very popular.

A woman is critiquing a painting while using a paint brush as a pointer. A student stands in front of her painting, which features a stylized cityscape in rectangular form. The University of Denver School of Art added additional classes that incorporated different styles and techniques under the direction of Vance Kirkland.

DU art students at the Chappell School of Art in 1956 are displaying art based on their impressions of the wood and stone carvings of South Sea Islanders. The students made advertising designs, textiles, prints, paintings, and sculpture. From left to right are (first row, on floor) Gary Kaemmer, Don Nordeen, and Virginia Kielhack; (second row) Pete Freyschlag, Warren Pulis, Kenneth Johnson, and Harriet Okamoto; (on ladder) Ona Ham and Jim Hendricks.

Civic Center campus buildings at 2011 Glenarm Avenue were used before new construction began on the 1445 Cleveland Place site in 1949. The gold dome of the state capitol building can be seen in the background. In 1947, the government center at 1415 Cleveland Place included the National Opinion Research Center, School of Corrective Speech, and School of Social Work, along with the Business and Business Management and Government Research and Management programs.

Howard Jenkins Jr. attended the University of Denver as an undergraduate and as a law student. One of his friends in law school was future Colorado governor John Love. After the March on Washington, Pres. John F. Kennedy appointed Jenkins to the National Labor Relations Board, the first African American to serve in that capacity.

The College of Law occupied half of the second floor above Mapelli Brothers grocery and meat market at 211 Fifteenth Street from 1926 to 1941. Howard Jenkins Jr., future governor John Love, and their classmates had to decide whether to swelter in the heat with windows closed or to suffer the aroma of butchered meat. The School of Librarianship moved into the second floor space in 1932. In 1941, the College of Law moved to temporary quarters

in the Mary Reed Building at University Park. Unfortunately, the students were no longer downtown near the law firms, and gas rationing made transportation difficult. When the university wanted to create the Civic Center campus, it acquired city block 42. Helen Bonfils donated a building and a corner with filing stations. John Evans Jr. donated the Mapelli Brothers building.

Law students are studying at a table in the library room above Mapelli Brothers. In 1904, the law school began the Legal Aid Dispensary, and under the Colorado Student Practice, students could represent clients in state courts. In the 1950s, students worked within the Denver Legal Aid Society. Currently, students serve clients in areas ranging from criminal defense to environmental law in the Student Law Office.

In 1959, the College of Law moved into the Law Center at Fourteenth and Bannock Streets, across from the Denver City and County Building. The College of Law remained there until 1983, when it moved to the Park Hill campus. This aerial view shows the Denver Art Museum, the Law Center, the Denver City and County Building, and West High School.

The Civic Center Classroom (later Business Administration) Building cornerstone was laid in 1949. The second floor of the building featured sundecks with tables and chairs. Students are shown socializing on the east side of the balcony. The city block acquired for the Business Administration Building included filling station lots on Cleveland Place and the Mapelli Brothers building on Fifteenth Street.

Students are sitting on the sundeck of the Business Administration Building during the 1950s. The Commerce Department became the College of Business Administration in 1946. The college was located at 1445 Cleveland Place from 1949 until 1968, when the Business Administration Building was built on the University Park campus. The Denver City Council purchased the Civic Center Classroom Building.

Well-dressed students are exiting the west side of the Civic Center Campus Business Administration Building in the 1950s. Cars are parked in the parking lot of the US Mint. In the 1950s and 1960s, business administration programs included accounting, real estate, management, marketing, statistics, hotel and restaurant management, business education, and transportation.

In 1960, students are reading the *Clarion*, the university student newspaper, in the Civic Center Student Union. The expanded student union, in a new building, replaced the Pioneer Pit, the overcrowded student union in the prior Civic Center Classroom Building. The new Civic Center Student Union had vending machines and a cafeteria, tables for studying and playing bridge, a social dancing space, and a juke box.

Two

UNIVERSITY PARK CAMPUS

The leaders of the University of Denver decided to find a pastoral setting for their liberal arts students that was more conducive to study. Wealthy potato farmer Rufus Clark and a consortium of farmers offered to donate 150 acres of land about five miles southeast of downtown Denver. Through other gifts and purchases, the new campus grew to nearly 500 acres. This was empty prairieland that had more jackrabbits than people, and electricity did not reach the area for 10 years. Trees were planted, but landscaping was not a priority until the 1930s. The first building, University Hall, was built in 1890 in the Romanesque style. Its cornerstone is one mile above sea level. A few blocks from campus is the Chamberlin Observatory and its telescope. Prof. Herbert Howe helped purchase and bring the 150-pound telescope from Cambridge to Denver in 1894. The 1893 silver panic, caused by the nation's move to the gold standard, came close to bankrupting DU, and only through the efforts of Chancellor Agustus Buchtel was DU solvent by 1906. Chancellor Buchtel was then able to erect buildings to join University Hall and Iliff School of Theology. On November 6, 1919, students from the School of Mines, a DU football rival, placed dynamite in several places near University Hall. The explosions blew out 100 windows in four buildings. Thick steel pins, covered with metal boxes, were added on the outside of University Hall to maintain the structural integrity of the building.

Prior to World War II, students came primarily from Colorado and neighboring states. After the war, veterans from across the nation, using the GI bill, pushed the university to over 11,300 students, the high point of enrollment. The purchase of the former Colorado Woman's College campus in 1982 almost caused the university to fall into bankruptcy again. There were major debts and deferred maintenance associated with the campus. Also, the law, music, and art schools required new buildings when the schools moved to the newly created Park Hill campus.

Buildings of the university can be seen in this sketch, but there are no other signs of civilization. The town of South Denver was created in 1886 but was slow to grow until DU began to sell lots. In 1892, the College of Liberal Arts relocated to the University Park campus. After the silver panic, the town of South Denver requested annexation by Denver, and electricity finally came to the area.

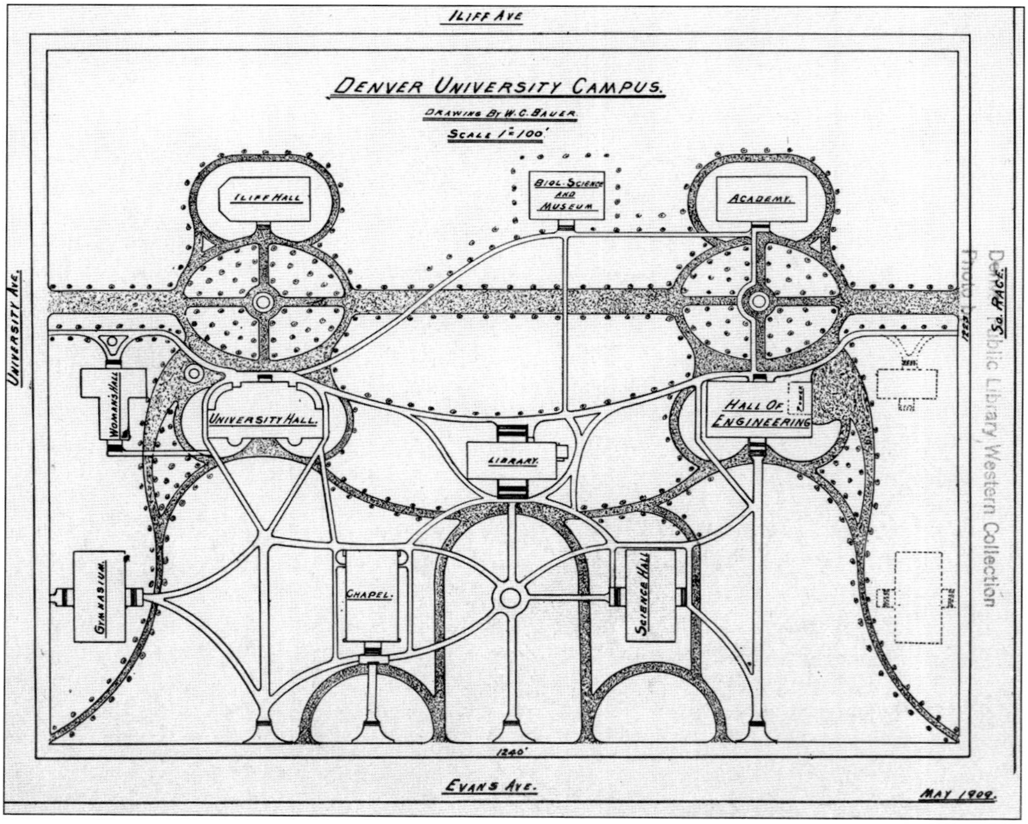

This 1909 campus map of the University of Denver shows the placement of the buildings on the University Park campus in relation to Evans Avenue, South Race Street, Iliff Avenue, and University Avenue. Although the university had sold much of the original 500 acres, there was still room for expansion beyond the original plan. The streets and avenues were not paved until the late 1940s.

University Hall was the first building constructed on the University Park campus. A large crowd watches as the cornerstone is laid on April 3, 1890, in the town of South Denver. For many years, University Hall included all university offices and classrooms, along with a library and chapel. It later became commonly known as Old Main and U-Hall.

Throughout the years, there were many dedications. The Hilltop Stadium dedication ceremony took place on October 2, 1926, on the University Park campus. Even after Chancellor Buchtel increased the number of buildings, the campus was still somewhat barren. For several decades, people had to tramp through high prairie grass and weeds with sharp stickers to attend ground-breakings and dedications.

The Iliff School of Theology and University Hall buildings faced each other and framed the expanse and the Rocky Mountains to the west in the 1890s. In the far distance, the newly opened Loretto Heights Academy is visible. Loretto Heights was a Catholic school for girls until 1988, when its programs were moved to Regis University, a Jesuit school. Colorado Heights University is now on the former Loretto Heights campus.

Before additional buildings joined it, University Hall housed virtually everything at the university, including classrooms, administrative and faculty offices, the library, the chapel, and a gymnasium. As evidenced by the hanging lightbulb, this photograph was taken after Denver annexed South Denver and electricity was extended to the area. Even when the unreliable electricity was working, only 12 to 24 volts of direct current was produced.

Faculty Row, in the 2100 block of South Milwaukee Street in University Park, was home to many early DU faculty members. Many of the early faculty were given land in lieu of salaries when DU was struggling financially. In addition to the silver panic in 1893, land prices had fallen dramatically, and the university's revenue from the sale of lots was depressed.

The Iliff School of Theology was built in 1892. The building was designed and built in the Richardsonian Romanesque style by the New York architecture firm Fuller and Wheeler. The Iliff School of Theology was founded as part of the Colorado Seminary (the University of Denver), but after a brief closing, it reopened in 1910 as a separate institution.

Looking west, the Iliff School of Theology, University Hall, and the Chamberlin Observatory can be seen in the distance. The Chamberlin Observatory was built blocks from the other buildings in what became known as Observatory Park. Prof. Herbert Howe was pleased that the observatory was in an area without urban lighting, which could interfere with stargazing. The placement of the observatory in the park shielded it somewhat when Denver growth reached the area.

This is a view of the University Park campus looking southeast at University Hall, the Iliff School of Theology, and Carnegie Library. There is a vehicle in the middle of the field, and the photograph reflects the lack of paved roads and sidewalks. There are few trees and no landscaping.

This is a 1912 interior view of the University of Denver's Carnegie Library. The large room contained five stained-glass windows, bookshelves, and a wooden file cabinet for vertical files. When a new library was built, Carnegie Library served as a student union and as a bookstore. In 1943, Carnegie Hall was remodeled as a large mess hall and post exchange. It was demolished in 1990.

The effects of the Great Blizzard of 1913 are evident in this view of Carnegie Library and University Hall looking east. A total of 46 inches of snow fell in Denver between December 1 and December 6. It remains the largest recorded snowstorm to ever hit Denver. Without paved streets, it took effort to make the university passable again. After the snow was cleared, mud remained.

Carnegie Library and the Science Hall were built while Henry Buchtel was chancellor. Dr. Buchtel, a Methodist minister, was a fantastic fundraiser, but raising money was the least favorite part of his administrative duties. He much preferred teaching. This image shows the Science Hall, Carnegie Library, and two towers of the Memorial Chapel. There is a row of cars parked in the prairie in front of the buildings.

Memorial Chapel, University Hall, and the Science Hall are shown in 1917. Students and faculty were required to attend services in the chapel through the 1930s. Although the University of Denver did not have a religious test, there were Methodist influences, including a prohibition on dance. Modern dance pioneer Ted Shawn was a DU student until he began dancing. Social dances at DU became popular in the 1920s.

At the urging of his friend Chancellor Buchtel, Andrew Carnegie donated $50,000 toward the construction of Science Hall. The building, completed in 1912, housed the departments of chemistry and physics, with laboratories, lecture halls, and offices. Students later called the building "the Gas House" because of the smells that emanated from experiments conducted there.

Electric poles can be seen in the distance from the chapel and the Science Hall. Electricity was sporadic, and the voltage was quite low. Prof. Herbert Howe wrote in his diary in 1890 about the "common loss of electric power in University Park after midnight, which interfered with the Observatory's instruments." Howe later wrote that the electricity did improve after a few years when the voltage was cranked up substantially.

The erection of Memorial Chapel was begun in 1907, but it was not completed for 10 years because of funding problems. The chapel was originally named to honor the memory of DU students who had died in World War I, but in 1948, it was renamed the Buchtel Memorial Chapel after Chancellor Henry Buchtel. This view is from around 1918.

The trees in 1930 have grown much larger than the earlier 1918 view of the chapel. The building style was Moorish baroque, and the front two corner towers were larger than the back two. The redbrick interior and furnishings were the gift of J.K. Mullen, a Roman Catholic, "in hope that religious prejudices may vanish from the life of all Christian bodies."

This photograph shows the Buchtel Memorial Chapel shortly after it was destroyed by fire in 1983. Only the southwest tower was salvaged, and it was renamed the Buchtel Tower. It now stands to the east of Anderson Academic Commons (formerly Penrose Library). The unproved suspicion was that arson was involved in the fire.

Mary Reed became a philanthropist after her husband died. When Carnegie Library needed to be replaced, she donated the funds to build the library that bore her name. Designed by Henry James Manning in the collegiate Gothic style, it opened in 1933. When Penrose Library was erected in 1972, the Mary Reed Library became home to administrative offices. The University Library Association holds used book sales in the building.

This is a pencil drawing of the Mary Reed Library building on the University of Denver campus by Jewish immigrant Alexander Kagan in 1948. Kagan received his art degree from the University of Denver. The drawing depicts two stories of the elaborate collegiate Gothic architecture and the southeast entrance to the library. (Courtesy of Beck Archives, Special Collections, University of Denver.)

Though the Mary Reed building has not served as the university library since the early 1970s, the original limestone library sign is still present on the front of the building. Many of the university's administrators now have offices in the building, and the formal Renaissance Room and the DuPont Rooms are used for receptions and meetings. According to legend, Mary Reed's ghost still haunts the building.

Patrons are reading and browsing books in the Mary Reed Library Renaissance Room in the 1960s. An unabridged dictionary sits on a turntable, and a male student is looking at an oversized book nearby. Denver architect Harry J. Manning created an *H* pattern, which allowed the three reference and study halls to catch natural light from the north, south, and west. Manning also designed the customized furniture.

People are reading, and others are performing research by using the card catalogs and the vertical files (filing cabinets with research articles) in the Renaissance Room of Mary Reed Library in the 1960s. Most current students at DU have no idea what card catalogs and vertical files are. A card catalog is still being used in the Special Collection and Archives in the Anderson Academic Commons.

In this 1930s aerial view of the University Park campus, the structures shown are Hilltop Stadium, Iliff School of Theology, Carnegie Library, Science Hall, Alumni Gymnasium, and Memorial Chapel. The gymnasium was built in 1910, after University of Denver alumni met fundraising goals and were rewarded with a building named for them.

Students gather in front of the *Alma Mater* statue near the Margery Reed Building for a photograph. The Margery Reed Building was completed in 1928 and named for the daughter of Verner and Mary Reed. Margery Reed graduated from DU in 1919 with an English degree and became an assistant professor. She married Paul Mayo, who also taught English, but she became ill and died at 31.

The Margery Reed Building housed the Theater Department, and this is a view of the beautiful small theater originally named the Margery Reed Mayo Memorial Hall. The theater could hold 300. The building was constructed in the collegiate Gothic style as designed by architect Charles Klauder. The Margery Reed Building is now being used for a variety of events and for offices.

The bronze *Alma Mater* statue is commonly called the "Mary and Margery Reed Statue" and the "Mother Daughter Statue." The sculptor was Sicilian-born Enrico Licari, who lived in Denver. The statue was funded by Mary Reed and dedicated to honor both Margery and Mary Reed. This photograph was taken when it stood on the central south side of the building, before moving to the Humanities Garden.

Templin Hall was constructed at the corner of Evans Avenue and South Josephine Street in 1907 for female DU students. The five-story structure was a dormitory until the late 1940s. The building was financed by Charles Templin, a DU alumnus, who sold Templin Hall to the university. Later it housed the School of Social Work and an English language laboratory for foreign students. It was demolished in 1979.

Built in 1892, Wycliffe Cottage for Girls was an early residence for female DU students. It was located at Asbury Avenue and Columbine Street. It later became home to the Phi Kappa Sigma fraternity and then served as a boys' school. Male students had to find their own housing. Most roomed in Denver and commuted to the University Park campus by streetcar. Some got jobs on the streetcars.

This room in Wycliffe Cottage for Girls, pictured about 1900, has a few pennants on the wall and photographs of fashionable women. The expanded seminary building in downtown Denver provided housing for both female and male students. When the liberal arts college moved to the University Park campus, there was no space for living quarters. By necessity, Wycliffe Cottage was one of the first campus additions.

Men stand near South Broadway Electric Line streetcars of the University Park Railway & Electric Company at Colorado Avenue and South Broadway Boulevard. Both an open-air car and a closed car are visible. There were no dormitories on campus for male students, and therefore most commuted from Denver by streetcar. For many years, DU was known as "Tramway Tech." (Courtesy of the Denver Public Library, Western History Collection, WH2129.)

Latin majors pose in a classroom in University Hall in January 1901. Latin and Greek were important to a classical liberal arts education, and Latin was also useful in the legal and medical professions. However, in the 1890s, the university started to move away from classical studies. In 1892, political history replaced Greek in the junior year, and sociology was required instead of Latin, which became an elective subject.

Grace Mabelle Andrews, a Latin major, is shown in her 1908 yearbook graduation photograph. Her minors were in French and economics, and she played the piano for gym classes for extra credit. The first African American DU graduate was Emma Azalia Hackley, who earned a music degree in 1900. She married an African American Denver attorney and organized the Chicago People's Choir, which included famed soprano Marian Anderson.

In 1889, four liberal arts honor students of the University of Denver, (from left to right) Elsie Meyler, Susie Hammon, Fred Krueger, and Malthie Loescher, are sitting in wooden chairs and holding books in a classroom in University Hall. Female students did very well in the liberal arts classes.

Twenty-three unidentified individuals stand in front of University Hall in the 1890s. Two of the men wear caps and gowns, one probably having just graduated from the College of Liberal Arts. The other man appears to be faculty. The Chamberlin Observatory was built in 1894, but University Hall was the only building where University of Denver classes were held.

Students from a DU sorority pose in front of Chancellor Buchtel's house, where they have been invited for breakfast, around 1900. Chancellor Buchtel and his wife, Mary, enjoyed hosting students and faculty as guests in their home. In 1912, the chancellor was given a rose bush from Colorado's western slope that had scarlet and maize blossoms. In 1948, the similar colors of crimson and gold were chosen as DU's official colors.

These 12 students were photographed in front of a portrait studio backdrop. The women have on fancy ruffled blouses for the formal class portrait. Male students wore suits and ties in classes and around campus. Female students would wear dresses or shirtwaist blouses and long skirts to classes and for athletic activities.

John Wesley Iliff was known as the "Cattle King of the West." His son William Seward Iliff, an 1838 graduate of the university, began the University of Denver women's drill team, which was composed of university students. In 1891, nineteen members of the drill team are lined up in front of University Hall. The women performed with their long swords with remarkable precision despite their long dresses.

The DU junior class of 1906 mocks the traditional senior class caps and gowns by wearing bathrobes. Many of the early students at the University of Denver were serious about their education, but that did not mean they could not have some fun. Chancellor Buchtel once had to postpone chapel services for 90 minutes because a junior class had removed all the seats.

The 1912–1913 University of Denver women's basketball team poses outdoors in their uniforms in front of a brick wall. Mabel Rilling (1883–1972) was director of physical education for women and associate dean of women at the University of Denver from 1909 to 1964. She was an advocate for active, physically fit, confident young women in a time when women wore bloomers, long dresses, and black stockings.

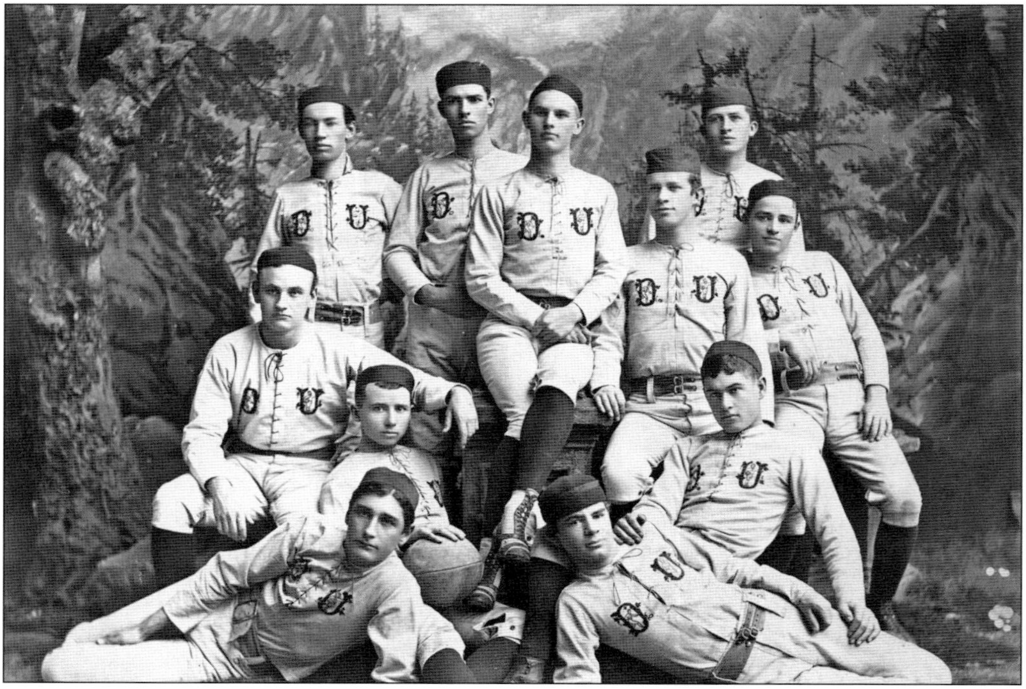

William Seward Iliff was a freshman at DU in 1884 and organized and captained the DU football team in 1885. The squad was made up of 11 men who played without the benefit of pads. Denver played only one formal game in 1885, losing 12-0 to Colorado College. The 1902 football team members pose for a group photograph.

A female student walks on a tightrope while holding a parasol for balance in 1926. In the *Clarion*, the image was captioned, "the straight and narrow." Memorial Chapel can be seen in the background. Students still use slack ropes, suspended between trees, to practice tightrope walking.

A University of Denver men's gymnastics team practices in the Alumni Gymnasium. The team also practiced outside. The construction of the gymnasium demonstrated the growth of sports and physical education at DU in the early 1900s. DU basketball games and gymnastics meets were held in the gymnasium for many years until the Fieldhouse Arena opened in 1910.

The University of Denver built a home for Chancellor Henry Augustus Buchtel just to the east of campus, off Evans Avenue at South Columbine Street, and it is still used by the university. It was often referred to as the "Buchtel Bungalow." Buchtel served as the governor of Colorado from 1907 to 1909, but during his term, he remained in the bungalow instead of the Governor's Mansion.

Inside the Buchtel Bungalow, students in graduation caps and gowns are gathered with Chancellor Buchtel and several professors. In the early 1900s, the Buchtel family's Jersey cow grazed in the pasture across the street. The university purchased the bungalow from Mary Buchtel in the 1930s. Able to hold up to 150 people, it is used by the university for small social events and meetings.

The 1915 DU faculty are sitting on the steps of Carnegie Library. Astronomer Herbert Alonzo Howe is seated in the first row at center. Ammi Bradford Hyde is second from left in the first row. Hyde was a dedicated professor of languages who died in 1921 at the age of 99. Both Hyde and Howe served as acting chancellors of the university.

In May 1889, students in Prof. Herbert Alonzo Howe's algebra class sit in front of blackboards. Howe spent over 40 years at DU, serving as both a faculty member and administrator for the fledgling university, and was a popular teacher. Mathematics was one of the areas in which Dr. Howe taught.

The seven members of the graduating class of 1894 pose for their class photograph. The graduation was just a year after the silver panic of 1893, when many wealthy families of Colorado lost their fortunes. The silver panic and the loss of land values again caused major financial difficulties for the university.

From left to right are H. Orlena Beggs, Charles F. Carnine, Nanaruth Taggart, Lida Burkhard, and E.N. Edgerton. These students were the editorial staff for the second volume of the University of Denver yearbook, the *Kynewisbok*, for the 1899–1900 academic year. *Kynewisbok* is an Anglo-Saxon word meaning "royal book of knowledge." Prof. Amni Hyde suggested the name.

In 1907, DU freshmen sit on the steps to the entrance of the University Hall. Most of the students were from the Denver area, but others came from other parts of Colorado and surrounding states. The student body increased from 640 in 1900 to 1,020 in 1910. By 1920, the university had graduated more than 1,000 teachers, 600 physicians, 200 missionaries and ministers, 600 dentists, and 350 lawyers.

In 1911, four adults and a large group of young students stand in front of Carnegie Library. By 1882, the University of Denver had a preparatory school for high school students and a junior preparatory school for grammar school children. The preparatory school was renamed Warren Academy in 1909 after moving into the basement of Carnegie Library. Warren Academy closed in 1916.

Herbert Howe traveled with the telescope lens to Denver on a private train and oversaw its installation in the Chamberlin Observatory. He was dean of liberal arts from 1892 to 1926. He also became acting chancellor in 1900 and again from 1907 to 1908. Dr. Howe pushed himself so hard that he fell asleep and missed seeing Haley's Comet in the sky above the observatory in 1910.

In 1888, amateur astronomer Humphrey B. Chamberlin donated funds to the University of Denver to purchase a telescope and build the observatory that would bear his name in Observatory Park. Chamberlin lost his fortune in the 1893 silver panic. Chamberlin Observatory, the small student observatory, and the Herbert Howe family residence on the far right are shown in this photograph. The dirt road later became Warren Avenue.

Dr. Howe chose the 1887 observatory at Carlton College in Minnesota as a model. The Chamberlin Observatory and a smaller student building were designed by Denver architect Robert Roeschlaub. The observatory is built of dark red sandstone and is listed in the National Register of Historic Places. Observatory Park is owned and operated by the city and county of Denver. This c. 1910 view is of the south side of the observatory.

Dean Herbert H. Howe stands in the Chamberlin Observatory with the telescope in the 1890s demonstrating the size of the telescope. A 5,600-pound tripod supports the telescope, along with a stone base that is 25 feet tall and weighs around 300 tons. The Alvan Clark-Saegmulle telescope lens has an aperture of 20 inches and a 300-inch focal length.

A man and woman stand on a platform that is reached by a ladder inside the observatory. The observatory has a main floor, a telescope room, and a basement. A pillar supports the equatorial headstock of the telescope, which allows it to rotate. The telescope is 19 feet long, has a tube almost 26 feet long supporting the lens, and is 32 feet above the floor.

Two women stand on the telescope platform to view a solar eclipse in a safe manner. There have been women astronomers since the mid-1800s, and women began studying at the Chamberlin Observatory in the early 1900s. Astronomy is now part of the Department of Physics and Astronomy at the University of Denver.

In the 1950s, four students look up at the sky above the Chamberlin telescope. Probably none of them is in a position to see through the telescope. Two of the students are on the platform that "holds 2 persons only." Dark-sky events are held at the observatory, and public nights at the Chamberlin Observatory began on August 1, 1894.

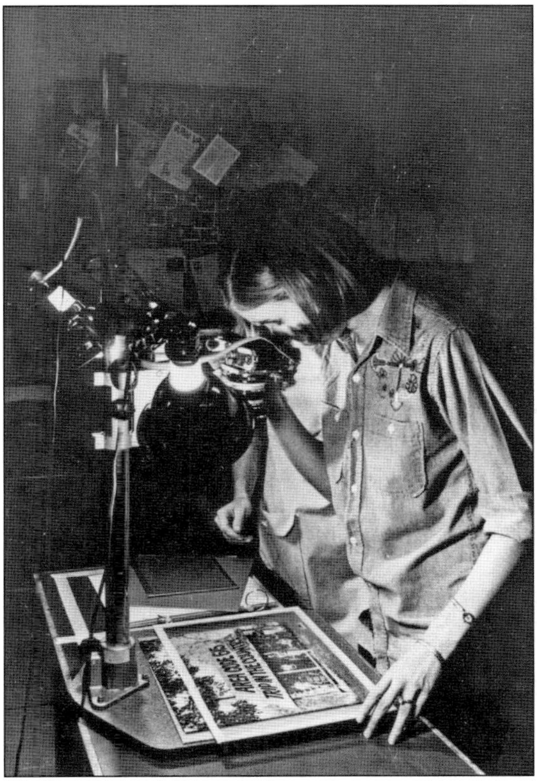

When the librarianship program was started, it shared the second floor of the Mapelli Brothers building with the law school. A School of Librarianship student is shown using a different type of lens to capture an image using a camera stand. Librarianship became a school at the University of Denver in 1931. The School of Librarianship Graduate Program was established in 1947.

In 1917, ROTC students participate in a formal dress drill near the southwest corner of South University Boulevard and East Evans Avenue. Etienne Renaud, founder of the anthropology department, was appointed the marshal and would at times shout out instructions at the troops in French. The Floral Building, constructed in 1909, is visible in the background. The building now houses Pete's University Park Restaurant and other eateries.

In 1952, five University of Denver students, members of the women's rifle team, aim bolt-action target rifles. After World War II began and male students entered the services, the University of Denver almost became a women's college. The students remaining on campus participated in war efforts such as war bond drives.

During World War II, many universities hosted Army Specialized Training Programs for teaching foreign languages. The University of Denver's Foreign Language and Area Unit was housed near downtown Denver in the El Jebel Mosque (Shriners). This image shows the Army students, faculty, and students at a tea dance in the gymnasium on the University Park campus. The dance took place on Commencement Day, March 17, 1944.

Three airmen are using the Air Corps Obstacle Center at the University Park campus during World War II. The Army Air Corps was one of the military units stationed at DU during the war. The upstairs of the student union (in the Carnegie building) was converted into a mess hall, and Templin was used as barracks. The School of Glider Flight and Construction began in 1942 and ended in 1946.

After World War II, enrollment at DU soared to a high of 11,300 students as service members used the GI Bill to obtain an education. Temporary buildings, Quonset huts, trailers, and old downtown Denver hotels were used for housing. This 1950 image shows newly built residence halls and post–World War II temporary Quonset huts near the corner of Iliff Avenue and South High Street.

These are Quonset huts on the unpaved South High Street where veterans and their families lived. Pioneer Village and Buchtel Village were two communities of veterans that were governed by the residents. The villages included 160 Quonset huts, 74 trailers, and 350 Butler huts. Married veterans with children had expandable trailers that opened out to form a kitchen, a bedroom, and a living room.

Two students are using the pipes in the basement of one of the resident apartments to hang laundry in 1952. Seven apartment dormitories were fully equipped for married students or for same-sex single students. The residence halls were used for offices before most were torn down. The offices had unusual configurations, but the bathtubs could be used for storage.

Carnegie housed the student union and bookstore until a new student union was built in 1950. Students are relaxing in the Knudson Room of the new student union on the University Park campus. The room was named for chemistry professor Clarence M. Knudson. In 1984, the student union moved into the Driscoll Center, consisting of two buildings connected by a bridge across Evans Avenue.

In September 1956, a freshman is entering one of the residence halls with her suitcase and wearing loafers and bobby socks that were popular in the 1950s. With her pennants and beanie, she shows school spirit during DU's Welcome Week. Beanies were given to all University of Denver freshmen.

During the 1950s, two freshmen are adding condiments to hot dogs. The students are wearing beanies and sweaters. From the 1930s through the 1950s, the beanie was worn by college freshmen and various college initiates as a form of mild hazing. There were strict rules for when and where the beanie could be worn.

This 1950s photograph shows DU freshmen in their beanies at a new student orientation picnic on the lawn outside Mary Reed Library. The freshman orientation picnic was a long-standing tradition at the University of Denver. An actual orientation picnic was stopped in the 1960s, but students still get together for a welcoming meal.

Students are standing and sitting at a registration table looking over paperwork at the University of Denver in the fall of 1956. Seven of the students are freshmen wearing their beanies. Student enrollment had dropped 50 percent from its peak after the GI Bill surge, but by 1956, enrollment had begun to stabilize. The steep drop in enrollment caused financial difficulties for the university.

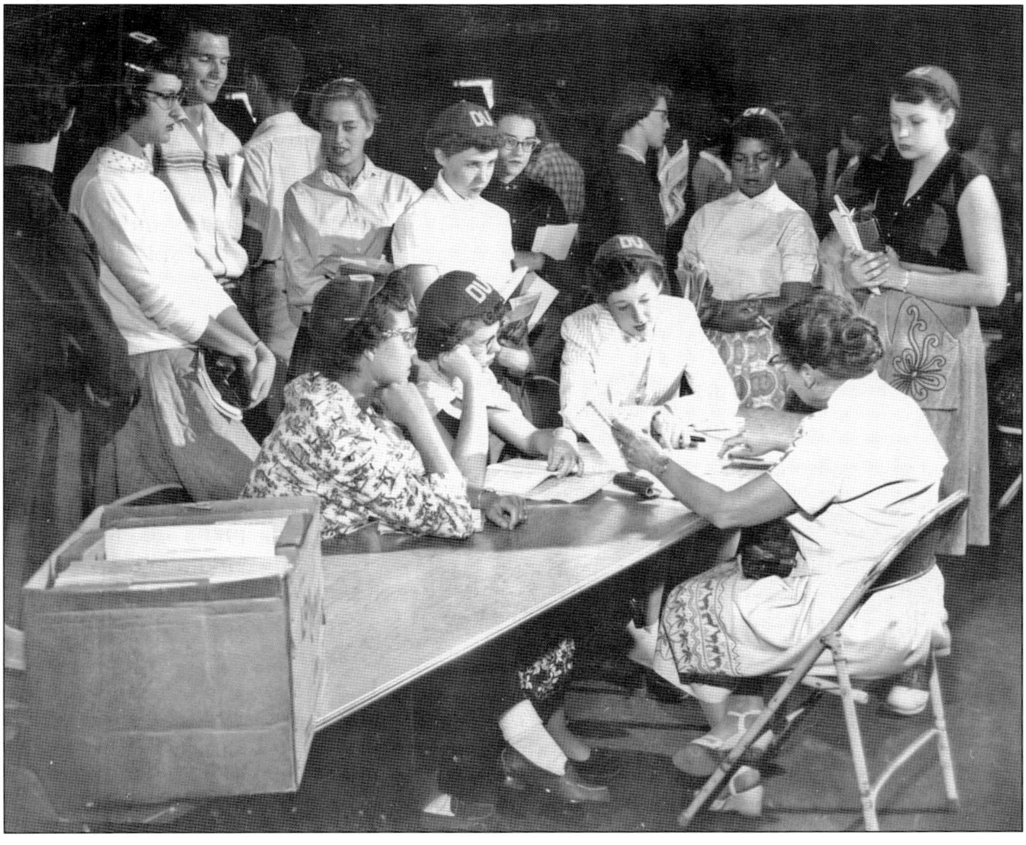

University staff try to help the large numbers of students who have finally made it to the registrar's table during the 1950s. To conduct student enrollment before computers were available, a large space was required for students to fill out the paperwork for each class. Registration without computers was organized confusion.

This 1950s image shows the interior of the Alumni Gymnasium at the University of Denver during registration day. The gym is filled with rows of tables labeled with signs either on poles or hanging from the ceiling. Students are lined up at tables with registration materials for classes in different areas of study and for graduate college.

Students display items for sale in the university bookstore in the 1950s. They are holding banners and other school materials. Various stuffed animals are visible, including a poodle, a long-eared dog, and a raccoon. Students in the 1950s bought many items that showed school spirit, such as pennants.

In the 1950s, students are purchasing books and supplies at the university bookstore in the student union built in 1950. The bookstore was in Carnegie Student Union, then in the 1950 student union, before moving to the new University Center. In 1983, the University Center was renamed Driscoll Center, and a new building was constructed on the north side of Evans Avenue to form Driscoll Center North and South.

A trio of DU students react melodramatically to Sadie Hawkins Day on the University Park campus. The American folk holiday was based on Al Capp's classic hillbilly Li'l Abner. On Sadie Hawkins Day, women can ask men for a date or a dance. (Courtesy of the Denver Public Library, Western History Collection, WH2129.)

This picture shows four University of Denver students performing a radio drama. KVDU was a student-run radio station that began broadcasting in 1947. The University of Denver also began Colorado Free Radio in 1964. Colorado Free Radio became KCFR and joined the National Public Radio network in 1984.

In 1946, twelve students are dancing on the west side of the University of Denver's Mary Reed Library building during a Dudes and Dames performance. The image shows the mountains on the horizon. The students twirl on the balcony of Mary Reed Library while wearing Western costumes.

A University of Denver student is reading a 1965 *Clarion* with an article titled "DU Wins in Overtime, Outlasts CSU Rams." The student has the bouffant hairdo style called the beehive, popular in the 1960s. The beehive was created by ratting (backcombing) long hair to create a tangled mess on top of the head, then carefully combed to create a smooth surface.

Dr. Margaret Fuller Boos was the first woman ranger naturalist at Rocky Mountain National Park. She established the geology department at the University of Denver in 1935. Dr. Boos was the geology department head until 1943, when she left to go to Washington, DC. She was dubbed the "First Lady of Petroleum" when she was a geologist in Tulsa, Oklahoma. (Courtesy of the Denver Public Library, Western History Collection, WH2129.)

Geology graduate student Lois Wescott served as a teaching assistant to Dr. Margaret Boos. Wescott is shown examining silicates in Rocky Mountain National Park in 1942, the year she worked on her thesis. She often hitchhiked to the mountains but said she always felt safe. After all, she always carried a very large rock hammer on her expeditions. (Courtesy of Women of Iowa Archives, University of Iowa.)

Ruth Murray Underhill was professor of anthropology at the University of Denver from 1948 to 1952. She was involved in the Indian Visiting Program of the American Friends Service Committee. She worked with the Tohono O'odham (Papago) and the Mohave of Arizona. Underhill lived in a log house in Denver and continued to write about Native Americans. She died one week short of her 100th birthday.

Byron Cohn and his wife, Essie White Cohn, received undergraduate and master's degrees from the University of Denver. He became the chairman of the physics department, and she became a chemistry professor. Diminutive Essie Cohn had to stand on a chair to write formulas on a blackboard. Here she is releasing a weather balloon to study the effects of high altitude on nutrition.

This photograph shows a truck in Farragut, Idaho, carrying the first load of trusses for the construction of the University of Denver Pioneers Fieldhouse and Ice Arena. The 94,000-square-foot naval drill hall was moved from a training base in Idaho. The arena was built in 1948 during the expansion after World War II. It was located where the Ritchie Center for Sports and Wellness now stands.

This photograph shows the arrival of a large Quonset hut at the University of Denver. Mary Reed Library and the Science Hall can be seen in the background. In 1946, the roads were still not paved at DU. Quonset huts were developed by the US Navy during World War II to be easily erected and transportable as the war moved between islands in the Pacific.

In 1951, students are participating in a geography field trip to a farm. Some of the students are talking with the farmer. On some of the geography field trips, students examined soil conditions. The students on this trip have equipment, and there is a large banner on the back of the Desoto that reads "University of Denver Student Fieldtrip Dept. of Geography." The geography department was founded in 1945.

The ground-breaking for the Johnson-McFarlane Dormitory at DU was in 1957, and the building was finished in 1958. Commonly called "J-Mac," it was named for two early DU faculty members, Granville "Granny" Johnson and Ida Kruse McFarlane. Johnson taught physical education at DU for 20 years, while McFarlane taught English for 33 years.

Cherrington Hall was built in 1966 to house the Graduate School of International Studies (GSIS) and is an example of International-style architecture. Chancellor Ben Cherrington, left, pitches a shovelful of dirt as Josef Korbel, center, and Chancellor Chester M. Alter look on. Korbel was the father of Secretary of State Madeleine Albright as well as mentor to Secretary of State Condoleezza Rice.

Ten graduate students of the GSIS pose for a photograph in 1980. Future secretary of state Condoleezza "Condi" Rice is seated third from the right. Her father became a vice chancellor at DU in 1967. Condi Rice earned her bachelor of arts degree at DU in 1974 and received her doctorate in international studies in 1981 with a specialization on the politics of the Soviet Union.

From left to right are Gene McKenna, social work graduate; James Kern, DU professor of social work; Edward Frieses, treasurer of the alumni association; and Sydney Rhea, board member of the alumni association. The Graduate School of Social Work was gifted an Olivetti Automatic Calculator for use by students and faculty members as an aid in compiling research data. (Courtesy of the Denver Public Library, Western History Collection, WH2129.)

Students in the Graduate School of Social Work take notes around a table during a small class during the 1950s. Social work became part of the DU curriculum in 1931 and became a department in 1942. The Graduate School of Social Work was established in 1960. Field work included working with people of all ages, from children to the elderly.

A home economics teacher is holding up carrots in front of a class of women in this 1951 image. The DU Department of Home Economics was established in 1946 and discontinued in 1983. During the Cold War, money was transferred from home economics to science departments. Beginning in the 1960s, fewer women were interested in attending home economics classes.

The School of Hotel and Restaurant Management was also established in 1946. Two students are learning from the chef how to cut beef tenderloins and filet mignon. After the apartment dorms were no longer used for residence halls, some of the buildings were converted for use as a hotel for the School of Hotel and Restaurant Management.

The YMCA and YWCA organizations were started at the University of Denver in 1896. The 1952 membership drive for the YMCA and YWCA featured "all the spaghetti you can eat." Ray Short is cutting up onions, Les Richardson is holding a paper bag, and Josie Elledge is preparing to cook the spaghetti noodles at the Grant Avenue Methodist Church in downtown Denver. The three students are wearing aprons.

A University of Denver student holds a double bass while performing a chemistry experiment. He is certainly multitasking, but it is not clear exactly what he is trying to accomplish. The writing center at the Anderson Academic Library has posted an enlarged copy of this photograph. Below is the question: "How would you caption this photograph?"

Biology professor Dr. Fred D'Amour conducted significant studies in the "Rat House" behind the Science Hall to help understand the physiology of humans. The "Rat House" was officially the Biologic Research Laboratory. He also studied cosmic rays and their effect on humans at the Mount Evans high-altitude laboratory. He loved the Rat House because he could work without interference, since administrators were afraid to come near.

A library graduate student is shown videotaping other DU students. She has an assistant to hold some bulky equipment. The School of Librarianship was established in 1932 and the graduate program in 1947. The library program was discontinued in 1985 but was resurrected as the Graduate School of Library and Information Science, which graduated its first class in 1999.

DU coeds pause on their way to a sorority rush party at the Senior Fence in 1955. For many years, the painting of the Senior Fence on the north side of the circle between University Hall and Iliff was a tradition. The fence was given by alumni to the senior class of 1916. A rivalry then developed between the senior and freshman classes over who would paint the fence first.

Nine beauty contestants, students at the University of Denver, are posing in a line around 1970. The students are dressed in miniskirts and are showing off their legs. Until the 1970s, there were selections of queens for Homecoming, May Days, Winter Carnival, sororities, and academic departments. The *Clarion* had weekly "Clarion Cuties." The May Days Festival began in 1913 with the crowning of a queen and a maypole dance.

Evans Chapel was built in downtown Denver in 1878 next to Grace Methodist Church. It was erected in memory of Josephine Evans, daughter of John Evans. It was later moved to the University Park campus when it was threatened with demolition in 1960. This view shows the chapel in its original location.

Originally, the plan was to move Evans Chapel on a flatbed truck, but the narrow streets and low-hanging traffic lights made that impossible. Therefore, the chapel was taken apart stone by stone, each stone was numbered, and then the chapel was reassembled at University Park. This image shows numbers on every stone. Surplus stone was used for parapets, walls, steps, and pools.

Lacy Bird Johnson, wife of Pres. Lyndon B. Johnson, helped plant an oak tree as part of DU's ground-breaking ceremony for Chancellor Harper's Humanities Gardens in 1965. Also participating in the ceremony were Chancellors Chester M. Alter and Heber Reece Harper. The oak tree became part of the Chester M. Alter Arboretum.

In 1967, students are walking on a path in the Humanities Gardens near the reflecting pond. Looking west toward the mountains, Evans Chapel is in the background. Evans Chapel was rebuilt on the axis between Mary Reed and the summit of Mount Evans. The chapel is used by campus religious groups and for weddings, memorials, meditation, and other services.

Ed Estlow (left), trustee Marion Gottesfeld (center), trustee Joy Burns (third from right), and Chancellor Daniel J. Ritchie (second from right) stand in front of an unidentified building site. Marion Gottesfeld became the first woman trustee of the University of Denver in 1953. She established the Women's Library Association (now the University Library Association) in 1956 to raise funds to support the university libraries.

Penrose Library opened in 1972, and $4.5 million of the total $7.5 million cost came from a donation by El Pomar Foundation of Colorado Springs. Penrose Library replaced the old Mary Reed Library, which had run out of space. One feature of the new building was that no windows opened. This was because students had sometimes thrown books out of the windows of the old Mary Reed Library.

Penrose Library was known for its "far-out" furniture. A student is pictured curled up in an egg chair after kicking off her sandals. Some of the chairs were retained, but the orange color has largely been eliminated after staff members begged for no more orange. The library was extensively remodeled and reopened as the Anderson Academic Commons in 2013.

Alan Swallow was an English professor at the University of Denver who in 1940 started the Swallow Press, best known for publishing literary fiction and poetry. In 1947, Alan Swallow helped to establish the Creative Writing program at DU and started the University of Denver Press, the first university press to publish new fiction. A man is sitting at a linotype machine, and two men are reading copy.

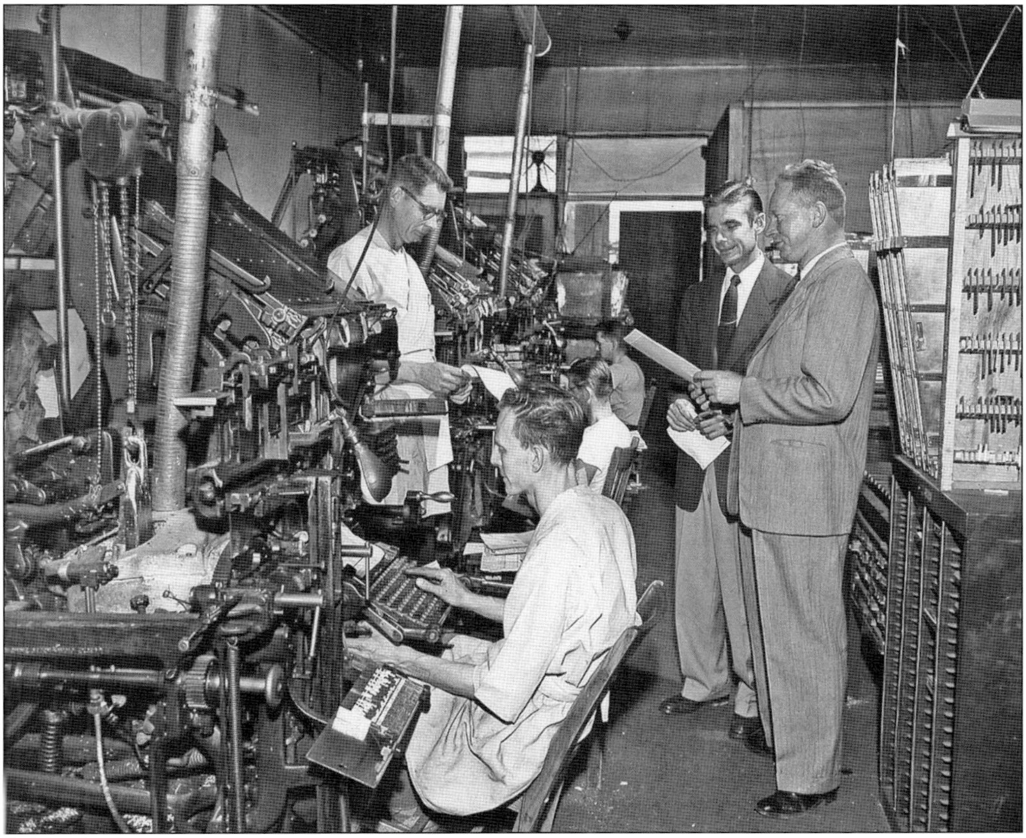

Hilltop Stadium was demolished in 1971, ten years after the last football game was played. It was difficult to demolish such a substantial structure, but this image shows how a wrecking ball was used to accomplish the job. At the beginning of the 1960s, pep rallies in the football stadium were called "demonstrations." At the end of the 1960s, "demonstrations" had a very different meaning.

A sit-in of 39 students in the DU Registrar's Office happened on April 30, 1968. They were demanding a student bill of rights, but Chancellor Maurice Mitchell quickly called the Denver Police to remove the students, who were suspended for a year. Chancellor Mitchell had asserted that the longest a sit-in should last was five minutes. Later, the chancellor regretted that he had failed to understand the students.

A large student protest that came to be known as "Woodstock West" developed on the DU campus for several days in early May 1970. Anti–Vietnam War sentiment and the killings at Jackson State College and at Kent State served as a catalyst for the protest. A convocation at the arena on May 8 drew 5,000 people, and construction began on "Woodstock Nation." The tents and shacks covered 7,000 square feet.

The Woodstock West community of up to 2,000 ate, slept, argued, and listened to hundreds of speakers, including Colorado governor John Love and leaders of the Black Panthers. Four hundred police arrived on May 10 and demolished Woodstock West. After the police left, "Woodstock West II" arose in the same location. But when the National Guard came on May 13, only a stray dog and a sleeping student remained.

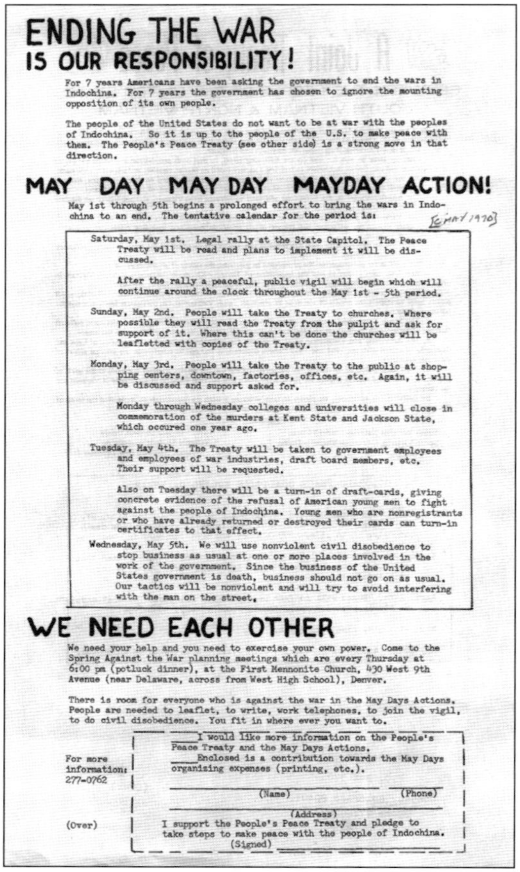

ENDING THE WAR
IS OUR RESPONSIBILITY!

For 7 years Americans have been asking the government to end the wars in Indochina. For 7 years the government has chosen to ignore the mounting opposition of its own people.

The people of the United States do not want to be at war with the peoples of Indochina. So it is up to the people of the U.S. to make peace with them. The People's Peace Treaty (see other side) is a strong move in that direction.

MAY DAY MAY DAY MAYDAY ACTION!

May 1st through 5th begins a prolonged effort to bring the wars in Indochina to an end. The tentative calendar for the period is: [c. May 1970]

Saturday, May 1st. Legal rally at the State Capitol. The Peace Treaty will be read and plans to implement it will be discussed.

After the rally a peaceful, public vigil will begin which will continue around the clock throughout the May 1st - 5th period.

Sunday, May 2nd. People will take the Treaty to churches. Where possible they will read the Treaty from the pulpit and ask for support of it. Where this can't be done the churches will be leafletted with copies of the Treaty.

Monday, May 3rd. People will take the Treaty to the public at shopping centers, downtown, factories, offices, etc. Again, it will be discussed and support asked for.

Monday through Wednesday colleges and universities will close in commemoration of the murders at Kent State and Jackson State, which occured one year ago.

Tuesday, May 4th. The Treaty will be taken to government employees and employees of war industries, draft board members, etc. Their support will be requested.

Also on Tuesday there will be a turn-in of draft-cards, giving concrete evidence of the refusal of American young men to fight against the people of Indochina. Young men who are nonregistrants or who have already returned or destroyed their cards can turn-in certificates to that effect.

Wednesday, May 5th. We will use nonviolent civil disobedience to stop business as usual at one or more places involved in the work of the government. Since the business of the United States government is death, business should not go on as usual. Our tactics will be nonviolent and will try to avoid interfering with the man on the street.

WE NEED EACH OTHER

We need your help and you need to exercise your own power. Come to the Spring Against the War planning meetings which are every Thursday at 6:00 pm (potluck dinner), at the First Mennonite Church, 430 West 9th Avenue (near Delaware, across from West High School), Denver.

There is room for everyone who is against the war in the May Days Actions. People are needed to leaflet, to write, work telephones, to join the vigil, to do civil disobedience. You fit in where ever you want to.

For more information: 277-0762

____ I would like more information on the People's Peace Treaty and the May Days Actions.

____ Enclosed is a contribution towards the May Days organizing expenses (printing, etc.).

________ (Name) ________ (Phone)

________ (Address)

I support the People's Peace Treaty and pledge to take steps to make peace with the people of Indochina.

________ (Signed)

(Over)

Anti–Vietnam War leaders in Denver called for a city-wide strike in this peace treaty leaflet. KVDU joined the national strike network, and faculty voted in favor of the Woodstock West spirit. Unlike many other universities across the country, DU continued classes throughout the protest. Chancellor Mitchell called the "village" a mushrooming squatter's camp but also believed that the campus should stay open to be a place of dialogue and discussion.

Two Colorado National Guardsmen walk with an unidentified demonstrator from Woodstock West in May 1970. Faculty urged students not to resist arrests by the police. Eighteen students and two faculty members were arrested. Some law faculty held seminars on the right to protest the war and assisted the arrested protestors. To ensure that Woodstock West III did not get rebuilt, police monitored the area until May 18.

The Woodstock West conversations included many ideas and events in addition to the Vietnam War. Students, faculty, and the public sat on campus lawns and discussed topics such as the civil rights and environmental movements. The group in this photograph is holding its conversation on the lawn near Carnegie Library and the Science Hall.

An anti-Wallace demonstration occurred in 1968 when George Wallace attempted to deliver a campaign speech in Denver. Members of the DU chapter of the Students for a Democratic Society along with other student demonstrators heckled Wallace so loudly that the governor was unable to make himself heard.

The university built the 25,000-seat Hilltop Stadium at South Race Street and Asbury Avenue to host football games and other major events. Alumni of the University of Denver had launched a bond drive, and William E. Fisher was chosen as architect. Hilltop Stadium would be a central gathering place in South Denver for the next several decades. Because of the rising expenses, football was discontinued in 1961.

A football enthusiast and member of the first football team in 1884, William Seward Iliff helped finance the stadium at the University of Denver. He died of a heart attack at a Homecoming game in 1946. The first game played in the stadium was between DU and the School of Mines in 1926, when DU beat Mines 27-7. The snow on the ground would turn to mud and make the parking even more difficult.

In 1998, the DU arena and fieldhouse was demolished to make way for construction of its replacement, the Ritchie Center for Sports and Wellness. Part of the student bleacher section remains to be brought down. The Ritchie Center includes the Coors Fitness Center, the Magness Arena, the Joy Burns Ice Arena, a 25-yard swimming pool, a soccer stadium, a stadium designed for lacrosse, and a sports medicine facility.

The University of Denver Pioneers marching band performs at halftime during a near-capacity night football game in a formation that spells out "DU" at the Hilltop Stadium. DU had 88 band members, four twirlers, and majorettes. When DU played Brigham Young University, the two schools engaged in a battle of the bands.

During the 1954 Homecoming celebration, students pose in a classic car with their University of Denver pennants. Homecoming began in the fall of 1925 and was briefly discontinued in 1960. After 1968, the Homecoming tradition became a hockey face-off between DU and Colorado College. Many Homecoming parades took place in downtown Denver. Homecoming is a time for alumni to come back and participate in the celebrations.

Two University of Denver Pioneers cheerleaders jump high in the air while holding megaphones in 1954. The megaphones were used to lead the football crowds in chants to encourage the team and to celebrate scores and wins. The DU Pioneers Fieldhouse and Ice Arena can be seen behind them.

Ruth McIntosh, the first female cheerleader, performs in front of a large appreciative crowd at a 1939 football game at Hilltop Stadium. She wore crimson shorts and a gold satin blouse. Until she graduated in 1942, McIntosh led the increasing number of women cheerleaders. By the 1950s, the cheerleading squads were primarily composed of women.

Cheerleaders are performing in Hilltop Stadium in 1955. DU's mascot was Pioneer Pete, and many supporters dressed in buckskins and cowboy hats. After football, cheerleaders continued cheering at basketball games. The last hurrah for Hilltop Stadium was in 1967, when the Denver Broncos beat the Detroit Lions 13-7 to become the first AFL team to beat an NFL team.

The panoramic photograph above shows a crowd watching the 1912 Thanksgiving Day game between the University of Denver and Colorado College at the old Broadway Park near downtown Denver. Broadway Park was at Broadway Boulevard and Fifth Street. Below the photograph are the words "The largest crowd that ever witnessed a game in Denver." Colorado College won the game. The photograph below shows parked cars outside Hilltop

Stadium, the football field, and the stands during another Thanksgiving Day game. This crowd is watching the 1927 game in which the Crimson and Gold of DU humiliated the Colorado Buffaloes 48-0. Some men are standing on top of cars to view the game. Parking in dirt lots could be challenging. Parking on campus is still challenging, but the lots are paved.

The University of Denver community is part of a large crowd intensely watching the football game in Hilltop Stadium at the 1940 Thanksgiving Day game. Although the United States was not at war yet, in October 1940, the first numbers were drawn in the draft lottery. Football and campus would change dramatically beginning in 1941. (Courtesy of the Denver Public Library, Western History Collection, WH2129.)

The University of Denver marching band sits on the field in front of a 1940 crowd. Physics professor Dr. William "Doc Hy" Hyslop led the university band and orchestra. After DU dropped the football program in 1961, the marching band disbanded. (Courtesy of the Denver Public Library, Western History Collection, WH2129.)

The University of Denver Pioneers football team fights for possession of the ball during a game at Hilltop Stadium against the University of Colorado Buffaloes on Thanksgiving Day, 1927. The DU Pioneers won the game against the CU Buffs 48-0. Not all the games were that lopsided. Unlike the grass fields of today, the football teams in 1927 played on Hilltop's dirt field.

The freshman and sophomore classes often participated in class fights during Homecoming. The fights included the flag rush, potato sack race, tug-of-war, and the ripe-vegetable fight. Freshmen could remove their beanies at Thanksgiving rather than at Christmas by defeating the sophomores in at least two out of three class fights.

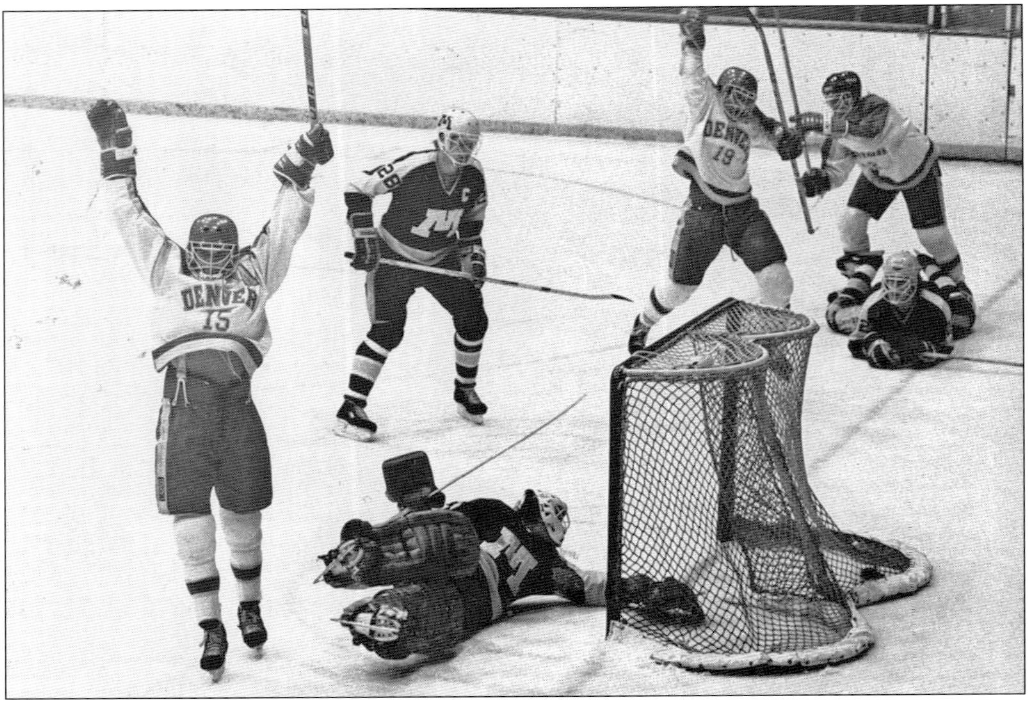

Members of the University of Denver Pioneers men's hockey team celebrate wildly on the ice after making a goal. Hockey games were played in the arena from 1949 to 1997. In 1999, the team began playing in the Ritchie Center for Sports and Wellness. After football was discontinued at DU, hockey became the DU fan favorite.

University of Denver Pioneers men's ice hockey head coach Murray Armstrong and player John McMillan lean against the boards in the DU fieldhouse arena hockey rink in the late 1950s. Murray Armstrong was the hockey coach from 1956 to 1977. While he was coach, he led the DU hockey team to five NCAA national championships.

The 1967–1968 University of Denver Pioneers men's hockey team poses for a group portrait. Coach Murray Armstrong stands behind the team. Team captain Keith Magnuson led the DU hockey team to become the 1969 NCAA national champions. He went on to play professionally for the Chicago Blackhawks.

Winter Carnival remains a very popular tradition at the University of Denver. Events are held at the University Park campus and at one of the Colorado ski resorts. The first Winter Carnival for all students was held in 1961 at Winter Park and included a downhill skiing torch light parade. The torch light parade continues to be one of the favorite features.

University of Denver skier Barbara Kidder poses for a portrait with her ski poles and goggles. In 1946, Kidder became the first skier, male or female, to win a national collegiate championship at DU. She was inducted into the University of Denver Athletic Hall of Fame in 1996.

It does not snow only in the Colorado mountains. A University of Denver student walks in the snow on the University Park campus carrying her notebooks and purse in her arms during the 1950s. During that period, women were required to wear dresses and skirts to classes, not jeans or even slacks.

Three

Colorado Woman's College and Park Hill Campus

Colorado Woman's College (CWC), now the Colorado Women's College, was conceived as a "Vassar of the West" by its founder, the Rev. Robert Cameron, who wanted to establish a women's college in the western United States that would offer high-level academics to women. The college was incorporated in 1888 but was impeded by lack of financial support. It was March 25, 1890, before the cornerstone for the Administration Building, later named Treat Hall, was laid. Money problems continued to plague the founders of the college until 1908, when Jay Porter Treat was elected president. The first 59 students arrived in September 1909, and the first commencement was held on June 6, 1911. The college was built on the open prairie in what became northeast Denver, four miles east of downtown Denver. There were academic classes, lively conversations, athletics, traditions such as the Hanging of the Greens, and time for fun. Other buildings were added to the campus, including Whatley Chapel in 1962 and the Permelia Curtis Porter Library in 1963. The tide of history was turning against women's colleges, however, and enrollment began a steady decline after 1967, when it peaked at 1,117. The college and its assets were acquired by the University of Denver in 1982 and it became known as the Park Hill campus of DU. In 1983, the Lowell Thomas Law Building was built, and the College of Law moved to Park Hill from the Civic Center campus. Alumni Lowell Thomas and Howard Jenkins Jr. attended the dedication. In 1985, the Lamont School of Music moved into the Houston Fine Arts Building at the Park Hill campus. The Lamont School of Music remained on the campus until 2002, and the College of Law left in 2004. Johnson and Wales University purchased the east part of the campus in 1999 and the rest of the campus for the 2004 school year.

Colorado Woman's College students had to "walk the plank" for four blocks from the main building (later Treat Hall) to Colfax Avenue, where they could catch the trolley into Denver. The entire area east of Colorado Boulevard was open prairie, and the ground was covered with weeds and thistles and was often ankle deep in mud after heavy rain or snow. Plank sidewalks were the only way to walk around campus.

An isolated Treat Hall is surrounded by snowy farm fields in 1926, a year before Foote Hall was built. Porter Hall, the third early campus building, was built in 1939. Treat Hall was located on a knoll on the open prairie. It housed not only the students and classrooms but all the administration of the college. President Treat taught classes, and Nell Treat served as the house mother.

The Colorado Woman's College entrance sign is partially covered with vines, and Foote Hall is visible on the right in this view. The sidewalk from Treat Hall runs under the sign, which was moved to the University Park campus after the Park Hill campus was sold to Johnson and Wales. The Woman's College changed its name to the Women's College when it moved to the University Park campus.

Trees and sidewalks are visible through the leaded glass design above the main doorway of Treat Hall. The cornerstone for Treat Hall was laid in 1890, but because of the silver panic of 1893, Treat Hall was boarded up and remained unused until 1909. The windows were boarded up to keep out the weather, birds, and small animals.

This 1940 panoramic aerial view, looking east, shows Foote, Treat, and Porter Halls after Foote Hall was built in 1939. Cars are parked along the driveway that led to the three campus buildings. After additional buildings were built on campus, the driveway was turned into a walkway. The same year this photograph was taken, William E. Porter presented to CWC a

seven-passenger Cadillac nicknamed "Leaping Lena." During World War II, student enrollment increased when parents became nervous about sending their daughters to a state college where there were so many military men. As part of the war effort, students bought bonds and collapsed large tin containers from the kitchen.

This 1913 photograph includes a group of Colorado Woman's College students. Jay Porter Treat, president of Colorado Woman's College, is standing in the rear on the right. President Treat and his wife, Nell, led the college through its formative years. President Treat taught as many as six classes a day.

The entire student body and faculty of the college is pictured on the south steps of Treat Hall during the 1911–1912 school year. Pres. Jay Porter Treat is seated at center in the second row. The boardwalk leading away from the building leads down to the trolley lines on Poplar Street.

Students and faculty in 1930 are posed on the lawn in front of Treat Hall. A portion of Foote Hall can be seen to the left. All the students are wearing dresses, as was proper for young ladies of the day. Until the 1970s, all students were required to wear skirts or dresses to class.

Faculty members Adela Zoe Wolcott (left) and Evelyn Green are sharing a secret. They were two of the first faculty at the Colorado Woman's College listed in the 1909–1910 yearbook. At the end of the first academic year, there were 3 sophomores, 17 freshmen, and 32 students in the preparatory class.

Two students are looking over the instructor's shoulder at a paper during an expression class in 1912. Reading books and great speeches was part of the courses. Before the 1920s, the Colorado Woman's College operated as a junior college. An expression, or speech arts, degree could be earned in two years. Music and expression degrees included courses in teaching methods.

The student staff of the first Colorado Woman's College yearbook (*Odaroloc*, "Colorado" in reverse) for 1909–1910 included Obie Sue Pulliam, Sylvia Kimzey, Orissa Hawkins, Bessie Lambert, Ruth Reid, Louise Hainbaugh, and Ruth Webb. The student body did not have the funds required to print a yearbook, so the first volume was handwritten.

Women in the auditorium in Treat Hall pose for the photographer. Almost all of them are wearing hats and coats and are seated on school desks because the theater-type seats had not yet been installed. Seated on the stage are 10 women and one man. Pres. Jay Porter Treat stands in front of the stage. Under CWC rules, a hat had to be worn when riding on streetcars.

Members of the Colorado Club of 1930 are posing in a *C* formation on the south steps of Treat Hall. Officers of the club were Helen Gregory, president; Margaret Hohn, vice president; Bernice Tunze, secretary-treasurer; and Merle Van Zandt, sponsor. Van Zandt is standing at the top of the steps.

During this croquet contest in 1909 in front of Treat Hall, Pres. Jay Porter Treat, faculty members, and students are watching Lula Pulliam swing the mallet. Croquet began in England around 1857 and came to America by the 1860s. Croquet can be viciously competitive when players try to knock their opponents' balls out of play.

In 1920, a field hockey game is being played on the barren area adjacent to Treat Hall. The area would later become the location of Porter Residence Hall. By 1920, students could wear athletic suits instead of long skirts. The CWC field hockey team often competed against the DU field hockey team.

Five students are playing basketball on the bare ground outside of Treat Hall before a gymnasium was completed inside Treat Hall in 1916. Athletic programs were an integral part of student life. The first basketball game was played against Littleton High School in 1909. The students declared it a good game, even though the Colorado Woman's College team was defeated 24-3.

Tennis was one of the first organized sports on the campus of Colorado Woman's College. Casual shirtwaists and skirts were the only concession to dressing comfortably to play sports. Outside practice was difficult on makeshift croquet, tennis, and basketball courts adjacent to Treat Hall when there was rain, which turned the ground into a muddy mess.

Helen Shotwell Bernard, a longtime member of the music faculty, is playing the piano. She was the initiator of the Christmas tradition of the Hanging of the Greens. She developed the idea while she was traveling in Europe and witnessed the ceremony, which was based on a medieval festival. The Hanging of the Greens was the longest-lasting tradition of CWC.

The traditional Hanging of the Greens is pictured here. The program was a dinner that featured garland bearers, Christmas music, tableaux, and a Madonna revealed from a triptych. The tradition began in 1930, when it was first held in the Gothic dining room in Treat Hall. This 1950s ceremony took place in Mason Hall. Guests at the dinner include US Air Force cadets.

Beauty pageants were a popular activity for the CWC students. In 1927, photographs of the 10 most beautiful coeds were sent to Cecil B. DeMille for the final selection, and he chose this image of flapper Elva Lundeen, making her the Colorado Woman's College Beauty Queen. DeMille was a founder of the motion picture industry and was one of the most successful producers and directors between 1914 and 1956.

Students are dining in Mason Hall in the early 1950s. The Dora Porter Mason Hall was completed in 1947 as a memorial to the sister of major donor William E. Porter. The Mason Hall dining room was used as a cafeteria when CWC became the Park Hill campus of the University of Denver, although night law students complained that the cafeteria closed long before their law classes ended.

This photograph shows the "bucket brigade" that was formed to move 30,000 books across campus from the old library in Foote Hall to the new Permelia Curtis Porter Library. William E. Porter funded the new building in memory of his late wife. On September 12, 1963, over 760 students, faculty, and staff transferred the books in six and a half hours.

During the bucket brigade, a student on a scooter is towing a bin with a library cart with oversize books. Another student is sitting on the back of the scooter with her legs in the bin, while a student in a wheelchair brings up the rear. When the CWC campus became the Park Hill campus, Porter Library was used as a library and for administrative offices.

Students Kay Nielson (left) and Dodie Gaeddert mix water from 33 states and two foreign countries in preparation for laying the cornerstone for Curtis Hall in 1956. Water to mix the mortar came from a variety of states and the territories of Alaska and Hawaii. Representatives from Iran and Panama brought water from their countries for the mix.

Essie White and Fritz Broman are instructing students in a science laboratory in the Huchingson Hall of Science and Home Economics. White later married Byron Cohn and became a chemistry professor at the University of Denver. Jay Porter Treat believed that the focus of a woman's education was to teach her to be a good housekeeper and mother. Fortunately, a bachelor of science degree was awarded at CWC.

Sixteen new CWC students, dressed in fashionable traveling suits, were met at Union Station in 1937 and greeted with a Colorado Woman's College banner. The dress code had been loosened, but students were required to dress for dinner, including wearing hose. Shorts were not to be worn except on the tennis courts.

Three students are enjoying a water fight next to the elevator in Dunklee Hall. The rules listed in the 1914–1915 catalog required students to learn the art of gentleness and stated that "boisterous conduct such as loud talking or laughing, romping through hallways, and heavy walking" should be avoided. The hall was built in 1964, the first of two modern dormitories on the northern side of the campus.

Foote Hall is shown after a snow storm in 1940. Three cars are parked on the curved driveway, one of them turned the opposite direction. This was before the number of cars on campus became a problem. Parking was very difficult to find on the Park Hill campus.

A large group of Colorado Woman's College students is getting ready to go skiing during the 1940s. Some of the students are kneeling in the snow and preparing their skis. Weekend trips to the mountains for downhill and cross-country skiing were a special treat for the young women of the college. The 20-acre Camp Freeman was given to CWC in the 1920s for students to have a mountain retreat.

Two students of the Colorado Woman's College are sitting in a prop plane. The one in the rear of the airplane has her hand on the rudder. The Colorado Woman's College had a flight training school at Denver's Stapleton Airport. Flight training was taught at CWC in the 1940s and 1950s. Some of the students became stewardesses, and a few became pilots.

In the foreground are the Porter Library and Lowell Thomas Law Center after the College of Law moved to the Park Hill campus in 1984. Whately Memorial Chapel, the Olinger Memorial Tower, downtown Denver, and the mountains can be seen in this view. Whately Chapel was dedicated in 1962 and the Lowell Thomas Law Center in 1984. Lowell Thomas was an alum who met his wife at DU.

Four

Mountains, Plains, and Beyond

Over the years, there was a migration from downtown Denver to the University Park campus. After the Park Hill campus was sold, the Women's College, Lamont School of Music, and the College of Law moved to the University Park campus and into new buildings. The University of Denver is best known as a major power in winter sports, particularly skiing and ice hockey. Skiing is also a major recreational sport for students. Under Chancellor Daniel Ritchie, lacrosse became a power sport at DU.

Northwestern University and the University of Denver were forced to come to terms with the role that John Evans, their mutual founder, played in the atrocities of the Sand Creek Massacre, and as a result, the first annual pow wow was held at the University of Denver in 2011. During the fourth annual New Beginnings Spring Pow Wow in 2014, Chancellor Robert Coombs participated in a special blanket ceremony commemorating the 150th anniversary of the Sand Creek Massacre.

Denver is known as the "Queen City of the Plains," but the mountains have always been an integral part of the University of Denver. The Mount Evans High Altitude Laboratory was built in 1935 near the summit of the mountain, directly west of Denver, at an altitude of 14,148 feet. The Inter-University High Altitude Labs (IUHAL) were created in 1948 as a coalition between several universities for the study of cosmic rays. The Mount Evans Laboratory was brought under IUHAL's banner with the creation of the university's Echo Lake Laboratory. The Central City Opera House was built in 1878 by Welsh and Cornish miners when mining was booming. The theater was saved from demolition in 1932 by Ida Kruse McFarlane, professor of English at DU, and Anne Evans, daughter of John Evans. They convinced the university to take title to the opera house and to renovate it and the adjacent Teller House hotel. The reopening production was *Camille* and starred Lillian Gish. A nonprofit group was organized and continues to manage the theater and hotel.

Mount Evans High Altitude Laboratory was created for cosmic ray studies. Over 20 cars are parked along the dirt road leading to the observatory. People are gathered along the road, and a few can be seen through the windows inside the laboratory. Atom smashers eclipsed the work of cosmic ray laboratories, but DU completed the Meyer-Womble Astronomical Observatory at the Mount Evans site in 1996.

Four female DU students, with a Daimler Mercedes automobile, look out over the mountain range from a Denver mountain parks road around 1920. Denver purchased land in the foothills and mountains and created a series of mountain parks. In 1912, the voters of Denver approved the purchase, and now, around 14,000 acres in parks, roads, and trails are part of the system.

Faculty members and students of the University of Denver sit next to railroad tracks while wearing hats in the early 1900s. Dr. Herbert Howe is at center, facing the camera. Trips to the mountains were favorite outings of the university community. Some faculty members had summer homes in the foothills near Denver, and the railroad was a convenient way to travel.

Red Rocks, another of the Denver mountain parks, is in the foothills west of Denver. The park contains 300-foot red sandstone formations. In this c. 1900 photograph, adventurous members of the university community are climbing up the rocks. During the Depression of the 1930s, the Civilian Conservation Corps carved steps and trails out of the sandstone and created a venue for theater and concerts.

The Aspen Institute for Humanities, in Aspen, Colorado, is shown in this 1973 aerial photograph. Aspen began as a mining town, but after World War II, it became a famous ski resort. The International Career Advancement Program at DU has annual programs at the institute. The purpose of these programs is to bring greater diversity to staffing senior management and policy making positions in international public service.

In 1956, Clifford Harvout (front and left of center) appears as Horace Tabor with Mary McMurray (as Augusta Tabor) and Osie Hawkins (as the footman) in the Central City Opera production of *The Ballad of Baby Doe*. Summer operas and plays continue to be performed at the opera house. Performances at the Central City Opera House remain popular, and people can view the "Face on the Barroom Floor" in the Teller House bar.

A man and a woman from the University of Denver ride a ski lift at a resort in the mountains on a clear Colorado day around 1960. Many of the faculty, staff, and students of the university are enthusiastic skiers. Members of the university community enjoy downhill and cross-country skiing, snowshoeing, and snowboarding.

DU Pioneers ski coach Willy Schaeffler and the DU ski team are on the slopes in 1955, when there were no ski lifts. He was coach of the ski team from 1948 to 1970, when the team won 13 of its 18 NCAA skiing championships. In 1972, Willy Schaeffler was coach of the US Olympic team when the Alpine women's ski team won gold and silver.

DU students and alumni have served in the American armed services since the 1880s. Several University of Denver alumni served in the Spanish-American War in 1898. Teddy Roosevelt's Rough Riders were made up of units from the Western states. This image shows Company M, Colorado Recruits, with alumnus Guy McCreery second from right in the first row.

Completed in 1933, the Phipps Mansion was named for Lawrence C. Phipps, vice president and treasurer of Carnegie Steel Company. The mansion was donated to DU in 1964 and was used for conferences and events for many years before it was sold. In 1997, dinner for world leaders in Denver for an economic summit was held in the dining room of the Phipps Mansion.

DU alumnus Lowell Thomas became a noted journalist when he wrote about spending 10 days with T.E. Lawrence in Arabia in 1918. This 1949 image shows Lowell Thomas and Lowell Thomas Jr. with three Tibetans in Lhasa, Tibet. Lowell Thomas and his son were invited by the Tibetan government to make a documentary film. They were the last Westerners in Lhasa before the Chinese invasion in 1950.

Staff and faculty of HERS (Higher Education Resource Services) pose beneath the Colorado Woman's College entrance sign. The sign was brought from the Park Hill campus when it was sold. The successor Colorado Women's College and other women's organizations moved into a new home in the Merle Catherine Chambers Center for the Advancement of Women in 2004. The original CWC sign was placed by the new building.

A little girl runs across the pow wow field at the University of Denver in 2014. There are rows of metal cones on her dress that jingle when she moves. When women participate in the jingle dress dance, the cones jingle in unison. The Ojibwa originated the dress and the dance, but the dance spread throughout the country, particularly after the resurgence of pow wows in the 1980s.

In this image, two men are in Native American dress during a ceremonial dance at the New Beginnings Spring Pow Wow in 2014. This was the fourth pow wow at DU. The leather outfits have bead, metal, and feather designs. One dancer has a very large feathered headdress. The men also participated in competitive dancing.

Tanksi Clairmont (left) and her daughter Wakinyella Clairmont stand in front of the Sturm College of Law's Ricketson building at the University Park campus during the pow wow in 2014. The University of Denver received the 2004 Gold Leadership in Energy and Environmental Design certification for the Ricketson building, the first law school in the nation to receive the green certification.

The first woman chancellor of the University of Denver, Rebecca Chopp, talks with DU students at an inaugural event. Sturm Hall, which houses the College of Arts, Humanities, and Social Sciences, can be seen in the background. Chopp became chancellor in the fall of 2014.

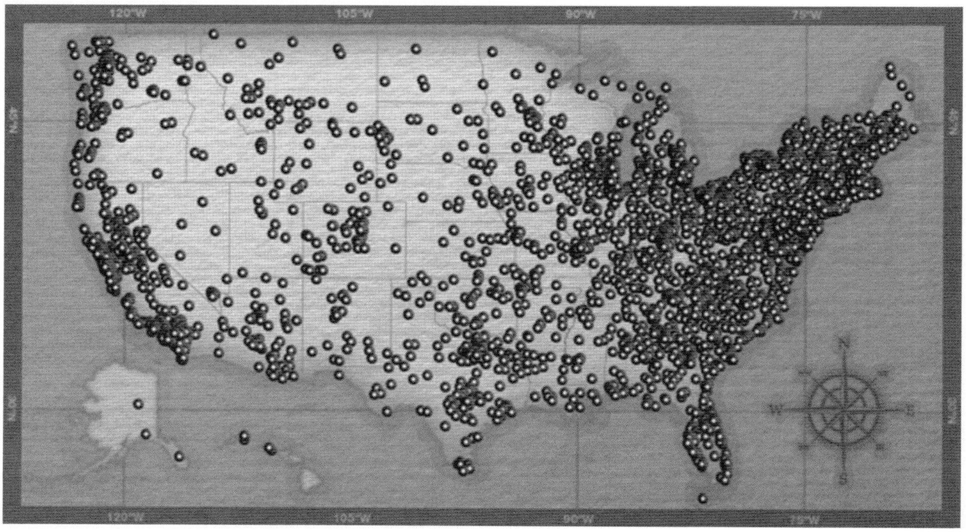